Learn Math While Drawin

MULTIPLICATIONS

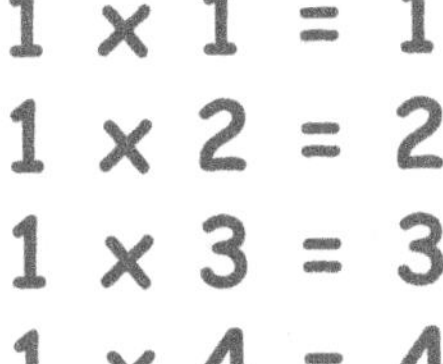

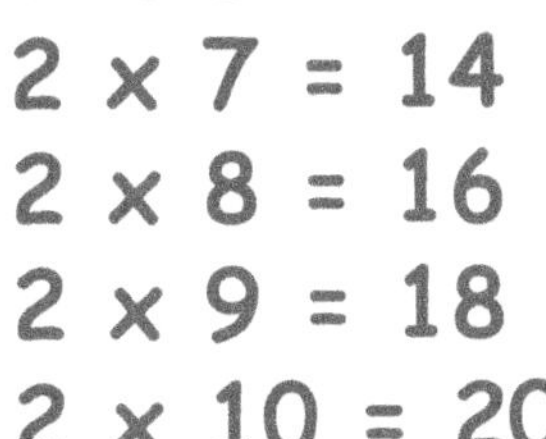

1 x 1 = 1	2 x 1 = 2
1 x 2 = 2	2 x 2 = 4
1 x 3 = 3	2 x 3 = 6
1 x 4 = 4	2 x 4 = 8
1 x 5 = 5	2 x 5 = 10
1 x 6 = 6	2 x 6 = 12
1 x 7 = 7	2 x 7 = 14
1 x 8 = 8	2 x 8 = 16
1 x 9 = 9	2 x 9 = 18
1 x 10 = 10	2 x 10 = 20

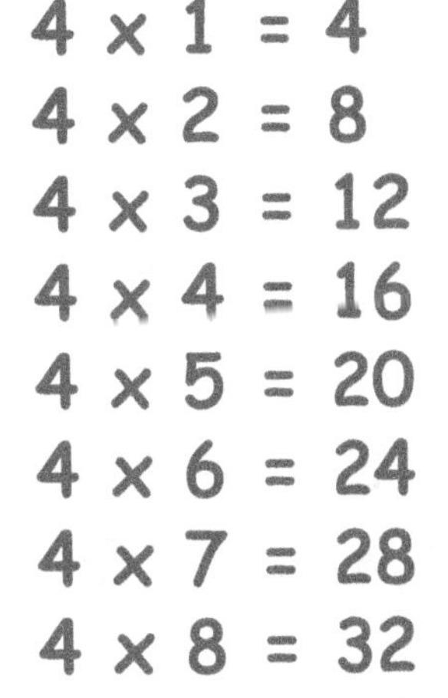

3 x 1 = 3	4 x 1 = 4
3 x 2 = 6	4 x 2 = 8
3 x 3 = 9	4 x 3 = 12
3 x 4 = 12	4 x 4 = 16
3 x 5 = 15	4 x 5 = 20
3 x 6 = 18	4 x 6 = 24
3 x 7 = 21	4 x 7 = 28
3 x 8 = 24	4 x 8 = 32
3 x 9 = 27	4 x 9 = 36
3 x 10 = 30	4 x 10 = 40

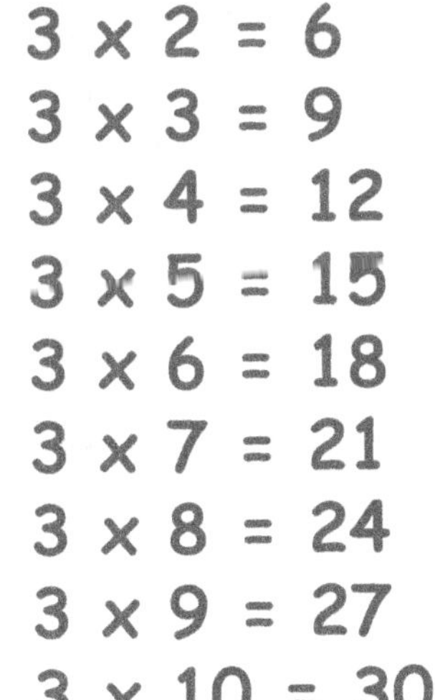

5 × 1 = 5	6 × 1 = 6
5 × 2 = 10	6 × 2 = 12
5 × 3 = 15	6 × 3 = 18
5 × 4 = 20	6 × 4 = 24
5 × 5 = 25	6 × 5 = 30
5 × 6 = 30	6 × 6 = 36
5 × 7 = 35	6 × 7 = 42
5 × 8 = 40	6 × 8 = 48
5 × 9 = 45	6 × 9 = 54
5 × 10 = 50	6 × 10 = 60

7 × 1 = 7	8 × 1 = 8
7 × 2 = 14	8 × 2 = 16
7 × 3 = 21	8 × 3 = 24
7 × 4 = 28	8 × 4 = 32
7 × 5 = 35	8 × 5 = 40
7 × 6 = 42	8 × 6 = 48
7 × 7 = 49	8 × 7 = 56
7 × 8 = 56	8 × 8 = 64
7 × 9 = 63	8 × 9 = 72
7 × 10 = 70	8 × 10 = 80

9 × 1 = 9	10 × 1 = 10
9 × 2 = 18	10 × 2 = 20
9 × 3 = 27	10 × 3 = 30
9 × 4 = 36	10 × 4 = 40
9 × 5 = 45	10 × 5 = 50
9 × 6 = 54	10 × 6 = 60
9 × 7 = 63	10 × 7 = 70
9 × 8 = 72	10 × 8 = 80
9 × 9 = 81	10 × 9 = 90
9 × 10 = 90	10 × 10 = 100

1 + 1 = 2	2 + 1 = 3
1 + 2 = 3	2 + 2 = 4
1 + 3 = 4	2 + 3 = 5
1 + 4 = 5	2 + 4 = 6
1 + 5 = 6	2 + 5 = 7
1 + 6 = 7	2 + 6 = 8
1 + 7 = 8	2 + 7 = 9
1 + 8 = 9	2 + 8 = 10
1 + 9 = 10	2 + 9 = 11
1 + 10 = 11	2 + 10 = 12

3 + 1 = 4	4 + 1 = 5
3 + 2 = 5	4 + 2 = 6
3 + 3 = 6	4 + 3 = 7
3 + 4 = 7	4 + 4 = 8
3 + 5 = 8	4 + 5 = 9
3 + 6 = 9	4 + 6 = 10
3 + 7 = 10	4 + 7 = 11
3 + 8 = 11	4 + 8 = 12
3 + 9 = 12	4 + 9 = 13
3 + 10 = 13	4 + 10 = 14

$$5 + 1 = 6 \qquad 6 + 1 = 7$$
$$5 + 2 = 7 \qquad 6 + 2 = 8$$
$$5 + 3 = 8 \qquad 6 + 3 = 9$$
$$5 + 4 = 9 \qquad 6 + 4 = 10$$
$$5 + 5 = 10 \qquad 6 + 5 = 11$$
$$5 + 6 = 11 \qquad 6 + 6 = 12$$
$$5 + 7 = 12 \qquad 6 + 7 = 13$$
$$5 + 8 = 13 \qquad 6 + 8 = 14$$
$$5 + 9 = 14 \qquad 6 + 9 = 15$$
$$5 + 10 = 15 \qquad 6 + 10 = 16$$

$$7 + 1 = 8 \qquad 8 + 1 = 9$$
$$7 + 2 = 9 \qquad 8 + 2 = 10$$
$$7 + 3 = 10 \qquad 8 + 3 = 11$$
$$7 + 4 = 11 \qquad 8 + 4 = 12$$
$$7 + 5 = 12 \qquad 8 + 5 = 13$$
$$7 + 6 = 13 \qquad 8 + 6 = 14$$
$$7 + 7 = 14 \qquad 8 + 7 = 15$$
$$7 + 8 = 15 \qquad 8 + 8 = 16$$
$$7 + 9 = 16 \qquad 8 + 9 = 17$$
$$7 + 10 = 17 \qquad 8 + 10 = 18$$

9 + 1 = 10	10 + 1 = 11
9 + 2 = 11	10 + 2 = 12
9 + 3 = 12	10 + 3 = 13
9 + 4 = 13	10 + 4 = 14
9 + 5 = 14	10 + 5 = 15
9 + 6 = 15	10 + 6 = 16
9 + 7 = 16	10 + 7 = 17
9 + 8 = 17	10 + 8 = 18
9 + 9 = 18	10 + 9 = 19
9 + 10 = 19	10 + 10 = 20

If you have 3 boxes and there are 5 toys in each box, how many toys do you have altogether?

____

If you have 2 bananas and each banana has 3 pieces, how many banana pieces do you have altogether?

____

If you need 4 packages of cookies and each package has 6 cookies, how many cookies do you need altogether?

____

If you have 5 friends and each friend has 2 pencils, how many pencils do you have altogether?

____

If a juice pack has 6 cartons and each carton has 3 juices, how many juices do you have altogether?

____

If you need to make 2 necklaces and each necklace needs 10 beads, how many beads do you need in all?

____

If you need 3 boxes of crayons and each box has 8 crayons, how many crayons do you need altogether?

____

If you have 4 shirts and each shirt has 2 buttons, how many buttons do you have altogether?

____

If a sticker pack has 12 sheets and
each sheet has 6 stickers, how many
stickers do you have altogether?

____

If you have 7 books and each book has
5 pages, how many pages do you have
altogether?

____

If you have 3 candies and they give you 2 more, how many candies do you have in total?

____

If you have 4 dolls and you get 3 more, how many dolls do you have in total?

____

If you have 5 crayons and your friend lends you 2 more, how many crayons do you have altogether?

____

If you have 2 apples and buy 6 more, how many apples do you have altogether?

____

If you have 10 dollars and you find 5 more on the ground, how many pesos do you have in total?

____

If you have 7 balloons and they give you 4 more, how many balloons do you have altogether?

____

If you have 2 dogs and you adopt 3 more, how many dogs do you have altogether?

____

If you have 6 pencils and you lose 2, how many pencils do you have left?

____

If you have 8 balls and you give 3 to your friend, how many balls do you have left?

____

If you have 9 books and you buy 1 more, how many books do you have altogether?

____